Investing In Art

16 Do's and Don'ts For Starting Investors

Urbain d'Oultremont de Saint-Marcq

TABLE OF CONTENTS

TABLE OF CONTENTS

INTRODUCTION

    What Is Art For?

    How Art Is Essential In The Personal Life

        1. It Fosters Creativity:

        2. It Offers A Total Education To The Individual:

        3. It Helps In Learning About Our Cultural Heritage:

        4. Provides Knowledge About Aesthetics:

        5. Projects Personal And National Identity:

        6. Helps Develop Subjective Thinking For A Cordial Human Relationship:

        7. Promotes Cognitive, Psychomotor And Affective Modes Of Development:

        8. Art Is Used In Correcting Physical, Psychological And Emotional Growth Deficiencies:

        9. Provides Avenues For The Development Of Cottage And Small-Scale Industries:

        10. Promotes The Tourism Industry Of The Nation:

        11. Art Reduces Poverty:

CHAPTER 1: INVESTING IN ART

    Special Considerations When Investing In Art

    Investing In Art Is Like Investing In Gold

    Is That A Manet Or A Monet?

    Buyer, Beware

    The Cost Of Owning Beauty

    Investing, Without Owning Art

    Protect Your Investment

    The Art Of Estate Planning

CHAPTER 2: CONTEMPORARY ART

    Shifting Strategies

    Appropriation

    Video Art

CHAPTER 3: A-Z TYPES OF ART

- Animation Art
- Architecture
- Art Brut
- Assemblage Art

- Body Art
- Calligraphy
- Ceramics
- Christian Art
- Collage
- Computer Art
- Conceptual Art
- Design (Artistic)
- Drawing
- Folk Art
- French Furniture
- Graffiti Art
- Graphic Art
- Icons (Icon Painting)
- Illuminated Manuscripts
- Installation
- Illustration
- Jewellery Art
- Junk Art
- Land Art
- Metalwork Art
- Mosaic Art
- Outsider Art
- Painting
- Performance Art (and Happenings)
- Photography
- Poster Art
- Primitive Art
- Printmaking
- Public Art
- Religious Art
- Rock Art
- Sand Art
- Sculpture
- Stained Glass Art
- Tapestry Art

- Video Art

CHAPTER 4: BUYING ART

　Tips on buying art

CHAPTER 5: MODERN ART

　The Beginnings of Modern Art

　Age Of Modernism And Art

　The Artist's Perspective And Modern Art

　Early Abstraction And Modern Art

　Modern Art Themes And Concepts

　Modern Art Movements

　The Avant-Garde And The Progression Of Modern Art

CHAPTER 6: HOW TO START AS AN ARTIST

　(1)　Practice Your Networking.

　(2)　Be A Well-Informed Arts Professional.

　(3)　Be Easy To Find. Don't Be Shy!

　(4)　Track Your Fans.

　(5)　Account For Your Art-Related Expenses.

　(6)　Broaden Your Fundraising Horizons.

　(7)　Catalogue And Document Your Work.

INTRODUCTION

Art is not, as the metaphysicians say, the manifestation of some mysterious idea of beauty or God; it is not, as the aesthetical physiologists say, a game in which man lets off his excess of stored-up energy; it is not the expression of man's emotions by external signs; it is not the production of pleasing objects; and, above all, it is not pleasure; but it is a means of union among men, joining them together in the same feelings, and indispensable for the life and progress toward well-being of individuals and of humanity.

There are many definitions of art, rising and falling in popularity at different points in human history. The loosest definition of fine art today is artifice: the creation of a thing, not by nature itself, but by the will of a person or group. It can be visual, meant to be seen; it can be music or poetry, meant to be heard; it can be a novel to read, a play to watch or a dance to take part in; it can be buildings or clothing; digital or virtual; it can be the disciplined training of plants or animals. So broad is the possible definition of "art" that some say one can make an art out of living life itself.

This definition, however, is not complete, because it includes many things people do and objects created that we do not consider art. So, what separates a painting from a carburator? Here again, people try to make a distinction through over-simplification: art is anything made, lacking useful purpose. This is also a fallacy, as fine art also serves many purposes, crucial to society. In more familiar terms, art is usually defined as that which was made in order to express feelings, communicate information, make a philosophical point, entertain someone, or beautify one's surroundings.

Art is differentiated from science in two ways. First, the definition of science and its branches are not widely debated, whereas art is. Second, scientific study relies on observation, experimentation, and peer revue, with one overarching goal - to increase human understanding of the universe. It's assumed that this will lead to a better way of life through better health, increased life span, more leisure time, etc. The effects of the scientific method are directly cumulative, with advances in different branches often coming together to form new insights and technology. While art also incorporates many of these same tenets and principles, it's much more chaotic, taking as many steps back as it does forward.

While scientists look for puzzles to solve concretely, artists search for a way to leave a mark on the world, to comment on it, basing their work as much on intuition (or more so) as on fact. Artists often look to solve puzzles that can't be answered with science. Often times, the purpose of art making is less akin to problem solving than to a gut reaction of the artist to his/her environment, compelling one to create. In addition, while scientists share their findings in a wider community, working together to build consensus, artists often find themselves alone, ignoring vast amounts of art history and theory they find objectionable. Even so, the two may overlap: scientists sometimes feel that their work approaches the aesthetic dimension of art; artists sometimes feel that they have explored their subject matter with scientific precision.

Throughout time, art has not always been made by individual artists, or even by people who would dare to identify themselves as artists. Some of the most ancient and profound art is "folk art," created by anonymous people under unknown circumstances. Folk art may be religious in nature - perhaps even an attempt to create a magical object. It may have been made by itinerant or untrained artists. It may not have been considered art at all at the time of its creation. Art as we know it today, is a fairly modern concept.

In the twenty-first century, the question "what is art?" has been debated for so long that, in terms of creating an art survey text, we now tend to accept Marcel Duchamp's inclusive definition, "Art is whatever an artist says it is."

Today, we also accept that industrial and graphic design are forms of art. These forms, like the old folk art mentioned above, were once not considered art at all. But now they have taken their place alongside painting and poetry; the artisan, or skilled worker practicing a trade or handicraft, is an artist if he calls himself one. And that means art can be everywhere--from the shoes on your feet to the car you drive to the teacup you sip from. We have functional art (objects you use) and art pour l'art (art for its own sake). We have "high" art and "low" art (whatever you wish those divisions to signify), high street fashion and Haute Couture, "real" art and "kitsch".

Today's world is a world of possibility and freedom. Although it is (and perhaps has always been) fashionable to groan that "true art is dying out", such a thing can never happen. As long as there are people who want to create, there will be artists. If you look carefully around you, you will see that almost every tradition and genre of art making, ever begun, is still going strong today.

The nature of art has been described by philosopher Richard Wollheim as "one of the most elusive of the traditional problems of human culture." It has been defined as a vehicle for the expression or communication of emotions and ideas, a means for exploring and appreciating formal elements for their own sake, and as mimesis or representation. More recently, thinkers influenced by Martin Heidegger have interpreted art as the means by which a community develops for itself a medium for self-expression and interpretation.

What Is Art For?

- The Product Of Conscious Intention,
- A Self Rewarding Activity,
- A Tendency To Unite Dissimilar Things,
- A Concern With Change And Variety,
- The Aesthetic Exploitation Of Familiarity Vs. Surprise,
- The Aesthetic Exploitation Of Tension Vs. Release,
- The Imposition Of Order On Disorder,
- The Creation Of Illusions,
- An Indulgence In Sensuousness,
- The Exhibition Of Skill,
- A Desire To Convey Meanings,
- An Indulgence In Fantasy,
- The Aggrandizement Of Self Or Others,
- Illustration,
- The Heightening Of Existence,
- Revelation,
- Personal Adornment Or Embellishment,
- Therapy,
- The Giving Of Meaning To Life,
- The Generation Of Unselfconscious Experience,
- The Provision Of Paradigms Of Order And/Or Disorder,
- Training In The Perception Of Reality,
- And So On.

This is the power of art: The power to transcend our own self-interest, our solipsistic zoom-lens on life, and relate to the world and each other with more integrity, more curiosity, more wholeheartedness.

How Art Is Essential In The Personal Life

Art plays a vibrant role in the personal life of the individual as well as in the social and economic development of the nation. The study of Visual arts encourages personal development and the awareness of both our cultural heritage and the role of art in the society. The learner acquires personal knowledge, skills and competencies through activities in Visual arts. When one studies Visual arts, he/she would come to appreciate or understand that art is an integral part of everyday life.

1. It Fosters Creativity:
Visual art education helps the learner to develop the ability to think, feel and act creatively with visual materials. The student also develops the ability to bring something new into existence. This desirable quality is acquired when the learner engages in practical lessons such as the designing and creation of an artefact in solving a problem or satisfying a need.

2. It Offers A Total Education To The Individual:
Visual art education offers holistic education to learners. Such education comes about when the learner produces an artefact in satisfying a particular need in the society. He engages in the organization and exploration of art materials, tools and techniques. Moreover, he gathers varieties of ideas, selects the key ideas, simplifies and analyse them, combine and separate ideas. These problem-solving activities help in educating the head (mental faculties) of the learner.

Also, when the artist uses the tools and materials he had explored and the techniques acquired in producing the artefact he develops manual or practical skills. This caters for the education of the hand.

Visual art education helps learners to appreciate works of art. When we see these artistic creations, they arouse certain feelings in us. Appreciation for the work would move us to talk intelligently and knowledgeably about it. This educates the heart. Owing to this, we can say that the study of Visual arts provides creative education of the head, hand and heart.

3. It Helps In Learning About Our Cultural Heritage:
Visual art education helps the learner to build an appreciation for our cultural heritage handed down to us by our forefathers. This appreciation is acquired through the learning of the various histories of art and the study of art appreciation and criticism. These studies help the artist to understand the meanings and usefulness of our arts which embody our set of beliefs and ideologies. Thus, works of art are used in maintaining the ideas, knowledge and beliefs of a society as handed down from one generation to another. In this way, we learn about our cultural heritage.

4. Provides Knowledge About Aesthetics:
The study of Visual arts helps learners to develop keen ideas about beauty (aesthetics). Since the learner is taken through a lot of appreciation and criticism of various artistic creations, he/she

develops 'good taste'. He is able to distinguish between artworks that are aesthetically pleasing and those that are not. This helps the learner to take decisions and make good judgements.

5. Projects Personal And National Identity:
Visual art education helps learners to build self-respect and personal ego. When an artist produces works of art in and outside the society or country, it projects his identity or makes him known to his own countrymen and foreigners. This largely comes about when the artist exhibits his artistic creations during art exhibitions, fairs and bazaars. When an exhibition is organised outside the country and the artist partakes in it, it assists greatly in projecting his/her nation.

Also, since the themes or subjects of works from Ghana lavishly talk about our culture, it helps in making our culture known to other people of the world.

6. Helps Develop Subjective Thinking For A Cordial Human Relationship:
Skills needed in building a healthy family and human relationships are reflected in art activities. Through the organisation of various opposing elements of design such as lines, shapes, texture, tone, pattern and colour into pleasant relationships, the artist is able to develop a peaceful and cordial relationship with people of various characters and cultural identities.

The study of art appreciation which teaches learners to develop the ability to see 'good' in every artistic creation also builds in learners the ability to accept people as they are. This subjective thinking helps in the development of cordial human relationships.

7. Promotes Cognitive, Psychomotor And Affective Modes Of Development:
Visual art education promotes the cognitive mode of development in learners. Skills in thinking and reasoning are developed by the organisation of materials into art forms and critically appreciating them. This critical thinking helps in the cognitive development of learners.

Practical activities in Visual art help to exercise the muscles and keep the body healthy. This promotes the psychomotor development of learners.

The affective or emotional development of learners is nurtured through the appreciation of works of art. Practical lessons in art help the learner in cultivating desirable ⬜ualities like patience, long-suffering and tolerance, which helps the heart to be always healthy.

8. Art Is Used In Correcting Physical, Psychological And Emotional Growth Deficiencies:
Practical activities in visual art can help reduce tension and emotional stress in people. The lives of physically challenged persons and social misfits are reorganised or changed when they engage in practical lessons in art. Those who have deficiencies in their physical and psychological growths are corrected gradually when they explore with art tools and materials in the creation of artworks. Art, therefore, serves as a therapy or medical aid for those with growth deficiencies.

9. Provides Avenues For The Development Of Cottage And Small-Scale Industries:
The Visual arts programme provides a creative base for the setting up of small-scale industries. Students are taught how to produce quality products that would meet the taste and demands of the market. In addition, learners are instructed in entrepreneurial skills and on factors to consider in the setting up of their own enterprises in the field of art. This training assists the learners in setting up their own small scale industries.

10. Promotes The Tourism Industry Of The Nation:
Works of art are sold to tourists to earn foreign exchange. Art souvenirs are exported to foreign lands to earn substantial funds for the artist and the nation as a whole. This helps in the promotion of the tourism industry.

11. Art Reduces Poverty:
Art is an income generating venture that provides employment for several Ghanaians. It helps its practitioners in earning money to fend for themselves and their families reducing the poverty ratio of the nation.

CHAPTER 1: INVESTING IN ART

Art has been emerging as a new asset class for the well-diversified portfolio. The reported returns are enough to catch anyone's eye: the index of fine art sales, used by art advisors to sell art funds, shows an average annual return of 10% over the past four decades.

Most people like to look at art, some people like to buy art, and almost no one likes to overpay for art. Yet that's almost undoubtedly what's going on in the hottest part of the market: postwar and contemporary art.

1. Avoid getting caught up in the hype. When any asset class performs well, more investors want a piece of the action. It doesn't matter if it's a stock, a piece of real estate or a work of art.

Recent art appreciation has triggered great excitement, but in reality only a handful of artists and artistic periods will generate those big returns. Investors can fall into potentially hazardous behavioral patterns, hoping to ride the wave when a certain asset class performs well. Buying that soon-to-be-discovered artist or that underappreciated art form about to become the next big thing often proves to be the exception, not the rule.

"When considering an art investment, it's important to step back and take in a holistic view of your investment assets, future cash flows and other tangible assets."

2. Think of art as you do venture-capital investing. Just as every start-up is unique, so too are works of art. Some have a track record of success, but many are prone to the whims of the market.

What drives passionate collectors is the individual interpretation and unique viewpoints on artwork. That subjectivity also explains why it's difficult to think of art as an asset class. Unlike start-ups, art has no balance sheet, cash flow or earnings to help determine its true value

To determine the fair market value of a piece of art, work with a reputable art advisor to find the sale prices of comparable works. The gallery or auction house may be able to provide documents showing their own related sales.

It also pays to learn about the artist's life and times. That information can provide context and meaning for an investment piece. Note any prestigious awards or fellowships the artist has won, academic positions held and notable collectors or museums with the artist's work. That information can offer positive indications about the long-term value of a piece.

3. Shun the belief that art sales translate to resale value. The secondary market for art is limited beyond works from "blue chip" artists. Also, before you calculate any windfall, remember the Internal Revenue Service considers art as a collectible — meaning the tax rate on gains is up to 28 percent. Add that to the expenses associated with acquiring, owning and selling art and you may net only 55 to 60 percent of the sale price.

Reflecting the wide spectrum of possible returns from an art investment, focus on non-financial benefits first. View any financial gain as an additional benefit rather than an expected outcome. And if you acquire art as an investment, especially if you're new to collecting, you'll likely want to work with a reputable art advisor.

4. Value a collection as more than the sum of its parts. This adds a layer of complexity to appraising a collection and raises important planning considerations for wealth transfer or philanthropic giving.

The IRS and others valuing estates after death recognize art as an important part of a portfolio, so make sure you've updated your estate plan accordingly. Do you intend to sell your collection before you die? Gift it to your children or donate it to a museum? Each of these options carries a host of unique wealth-transfer and tax implications.

Special Considerations When Investing In Art

Art can be a tempting investment, with its creative mystique and potential for soaring values. Attending glittering events such as the annual Art Basel Miami Beach, a four-day, celebrity-studded event representing more than 2,000 contemporary artists, makes it that much harder to resist.

Whether your tastes are classic or avant-garde, art is a tangible commodity and, as with any commodity, many investors view it as a hedge against stock market volatility. But before you drop a bundle at a gallery or raise your bidding paddle at auction, understand that art comes with its own risks and expenses.

Aside from the added costs associated with maintaining art, there are the fickle tastes of buyers. "Art follows fashions and trends," says Dorit Straus, worldwide fine art manager at Chubb Group of Insurance Companies. The popularity of various artists and periods fluctuate, so one year's must-have Andy Warhol is another year's Monet.

Having said that, Straus says art investing can be lucrative."If you take a long view of art, many investors have reaped the benefits, but you have to buy right and know what you're buying."

Investing In Art Is Like Investing In Gold

Adding art to your portfolio could reap financial benefits in the long term, but you need to understand how it fits in with your other investments.

Investors shouldn't think of art as just another commodity, like gold, for instance. "It's much more nuanced than that," says Jeff Rabin, co-founder and principal of Artvest Partners LLC, an advisory firm for art investors. "I tell clients it's the most opaque, illiquid and unregulated asset."

Given those limitations, Rabin counsels investors to take care of their liquid asset needs before buying art and to build a cash cushion for market downturns. In 2008 and 2009, collectors were selling what Rabin calls "phenomenal works of art" on the cheap in order to raise cash. That may be good for buyers, but it will put a major dent in your long-term portfolio if you're the seller.

Because art comes with so many investment risks, most likely you'll need specific advice from an expert. "Investing in art is much more complicated than people realize," Rabin says. "Just because you're talented in other areas of investing doesn't mean you'll excel in art."

Is That A Manet Or A Monet?

Buying any collectible with a long and varied history is not easy. One artist may have several different periods, some more valuable than others.

Purchasing art as an investment requires a somewhat contrarian viewpoint. "If a work of art is considered 'hot,' it's going to be fully priced," says Rabin. "I would caution investors to look beyond what everyone else is chasing."

The art world is also fraught with fraud, making due diligence a priority. The provenance, or origin, of a work of art is essential. But sometimes if a deal looks too neat and clean, especially if it's an old master, it could be a scam. "The more paperwork and data someone is providing, the more suspicious you should be," Rabin says. "And anytime anyone pulls out a Rembrandt or a Raphael, you should run."

Artvest also developed an educational nonprofit website, ArtInvestmentCouncil.com, covering all aspects of art investment, which can be a helpful tool for beginning investors.

Buyer, Beware

How easy is it for an art-lover to walk into a gallery and buy a piece of art? "I wouldn't liken it to any other industry," says Rabin. There are a lot of variables to buying art. Whether or not you can negotiate prices, for instance, depends on the gallery, the popularity of the artist, the condition of the work and many other factors.

An art adviser can help navigate the purchase, but you need to do some research there, too, Rabin says, by making sure the adviser is one you can trust, with pricing that is transparent. Make sure he or she is only paid by you and not receiving fees from a gallery.

Before you stroll into a gallery or art fair, take the time to educate yourself. Rabin recommends reading art publications, visiting galleries and attending events such as Art Basel. "Get familiar with different periods and genres, talk to artists, visit galleries," he says. "Don't buy anything until you've researched the artist."

Even if you aren't able to afford what the top dealers are offering, at least know what they are showing, says Straus. That will give you an idea of what's selling. "The key is to talk to everyone," she adds.

The Cost Of Owning Beauty

There are several costs associated with owning art that you won't have with other investments, says Straus. They include regular appraisals, storage, insurance, maintenance, and auction or gallery fees.

Art is subject to all sorts of risks that affect its physical condition and if you want it to maintain its value, it has to stay pristine. And that involves costs. "Art is not like stocks and bonds that you can put in a bank safe," says Straus.

Taxes are another consideration because they could be higher than they would be on a portfolio of stocks or bonds. Art is considered a collectible, and generally will be taxed at the higher capital gains rate of 28 percent, versus the current 15 percent for most equities held long term. The rate could be even higher if you sell the art within a year because gains will be taxed as ordinary income.

Investing, Without Owning Art

If you want to include art in your portfolio purely for investment purposes, without the challenges of owning a physical collection, consider an art fund. In such a fund, investors get much more diversification than they could from amassing a physical collection, according to Rabin, but they don't need to have all the expertise, or worry about storage, restoration, transportation, security and insurance issues.

There are different types of funds with diverse investing strategies. Some are opportunistic, with managers looking across the art world for any good investments. Others are more specific, specializing in certain periods, regions or artists. So, shop around for the one that is appropriate for your portfolio.

Be aware that art funds usually have no liquidity and long holding periods — eight years is typical, says Rabin. In order for funds to gain returns from investments, the managers need the time to invest the assets and the choice to liquidate them over time. "In that respect they should be thought of more like a private equity fund than a mutual fund," he says.

Protect Your Investment

Insurance for works of art is surprisingly inexpensive, relative to jewelry or other collectibles, says Straus, but it's one of the best investments a collector can make. A regular homeowners insurance policy will not be sufficient and serious investors should find a company that specializes in the specific type of art they collect.

Most fine art policies don't have deductibles, but look for a scheduled, all-risk policy with very few exclusions that will reflect the current value of the artwork, Straus says.

But a good insurance company can do more than provide a policy. Representatives will come to your home and review where your paintings are installed — for instance, over a working fireplace is a no-no because of the possibility of soot — how they are hung and stored, and the general environment. In Florida, humidity is a problem, especially for works of art hung outside, Straus says. Some works of art are susceptible to sunlight, but special glass coverings can help protect them. The company can also make suggestions about how to frame art and maintain it.

The company should also be able to help provide a raft of resources to maintain and protect your collection. Chubb developed its Masterpiece Protection Network of packers, movers, storage facilities, appraisers and "everything to do with art," which is continually updated and provided to clients, says Straus.

The Art Of Estate Planning

Bequeathing an intact collection to heirs can leave them with a huge tax bill and a difficult asset to manage and sell. Advance estate planning is essential because the potential for appreciation could quickly put an owner over the federal estate tax limits.

Even if you think you can avoid taxes by leaving the collection to a museum upon your death, you should make sure the deal is inked well in advance. "Often a museum is not looking for an entire collection, or there may be works or artists that are not desirable to a museum's collection," says Rabin.

One of the best ways to avoid estate taxes upon your death is to put the art inside certain trusts. An attorney can help you decide which works best for saving taxes and preserving a collection and its appreciation for a charity or family.

CHAPTER 2: CONTEMPORARY ART

To many people, coming up with a contemporary art definition can be a troublesome task. While its title is simplistic and straightforward, its modern-day meaning is not as clear-cut. Fortunately, understanding what constitutes as "contemporary" is entirely possible once one traces the concept's history and explores its underlying themes.

Contemporary art is notoriously difficult to understand and can be quite intimidating. For one, unlike past movements, the range of artistic styles of the present haven't been digested by critics, curators, and art historians and don't lend themselves to easy categorization.

In its most basic sense, the term contemporary art refers to art namely, painting, sculpture, photography, installation, performance, and video art produced today. Though seemingly simple, the details surrounding this definition are often a bit fuzzy, as different individuals' interpretations of "today" may widely and wildly vary. Therefore, the exact starting point of the genre is still debated; however, many art historians consider the late 1960s (the end of modern art, or modernism) to be an adequate estimate.

Strictly speaking, the term "contemporary art" refers to art made and produced by artists living today. Today's artists work in and respond to a global environment that is culturally diverse, technologically advancing, and multifaceted. Working in a wide range of mediums, contemporary artists often reflect and comment on modern-day society. When engaging with contemporary art, viewers are challenged to set aside questions such as, "Is a work of art good?" or "Is the work aesthetically pleasing?" Instead, viewers consider whether art is "challenging" or "interesting." Contemporary artists may question traditional ideas of how art is defined, what constitutes art, and how art is made, while creating a dialogue with and in some cases rejecting the styles and movements that came before them.

Since the early 20th century, some artists have turned away from realistic representation and the depiction of the human figure, and have moved increasingly towards abstraction. In New York City after World War II, the art world coined the term "abstract expressionism" to characterize an art movement that was neither completely abstract, nor expressionistic. Nevertheless, the movement challenged artists to place more emphasis on the process of making art rather than the final product. Artists like Jackson Pollock brought art-making to choreographic heights by dripping paint in grand yet spontaneous gestures. As one critic noted, the canvas was an arena in which to act "what was going on in the canvas was not a picture but an event." This notion of art as an event emerged out of the movement called abstract expressionism, which greatly influenced the art movements that followed, and continues to inspire artists living today.

Contemporary artists working within the postmodern movement reject the concept of mainstream art and embrace the notion of "artistic pluralism," the acceptance of a variety of artistic intentions and styles. Whether influenced by or grounded in performance art, pop art, Minimalism, conceptual art, or video, contemporary artists pull from an infinite variety of materials, sources, and styles to create art. For this reason, it is difficult to briefly summarize and accurately reflect the complexity of concepts and materials used by contemporary artists. This overview highlights a few of the contemporary artists whose work is on view at the Getty Museum and the concepts they explore in their work.

Contemporary artists continue to use a varied vocabulary of abstract and representational forms to convey their ideas. It is important to remember that the art of our time did not develop in a vacuum; rather, it reflects the social and political concerns of its cultural context. For example, artists like Judy Chicago, who were inspired by the feminist movement of the early 1970s, embraced imagery and art forms that had historical connections to women.

In the 1980s, artists appropriated the style and methods of mass media advertising to investigate issues of cultural authority and identity politics. More recently, artists like Maya Lin, who designed the Vietnam Veterans' Memorial Wall in Washington D.C., and Richard Serra, who was loosely associated with Minimalism in the 1960s, have adapted characteristics of Minimalist art to create new abstract sculptures that encourage more personal interaction and emotional response among viewers.

Shifting Strategies

Minimalism and Pop Art paved the way for later artists to explore questions about the conceptual nature of art, its form, its production, and its ability to communicate in different ways. In the late 1960s and 1970s, these ideas led to a "dematerialization of art," when artists turned away from painting and sculpture to experiment with new formats including photography, film and video, performance art, large-scale installations and earth works. Although some critics of the time foretold "the death of painting," art today encompasses a broad range of traditional and experimental media, including works that rely on Internet technology and other scientific innovations.

These shifting strategies to engage the viewer show how contemporary art's significance exists beyond the object itself. Its meaning develops from cultural discourse, interpretation and a range of individual understandings, in addition to the formal and conceptual problems that first motivated the artist. In this way, the art of our times may serve as a catalyst for an on-going process of open discussion and intellectual inquiry about the world today.

Appropriation

Contemporary artists, like many artists that preceded them, may acknowledge and find inspiration in art works from previous time periods in both subject matter and formal elements. Sometimes this inspiration takes the form of appropriation. Artist John Baldessari "borrowed" an image from 1505 of a stag beetle by the German artist Albrecht Dürer and made it his own. Using modern-day materials (ink-jet printing mounted on a fiberglass panel), Baldessari juxtaposed the original image with a piece of sculpture in the form of a giant steel pin. By inserting the steel pin into the canvas, Baldessari combines mediums in a very modern way.

Video Art

In the 1960s, artists began to turn to the medium of video to redefine fine art. Through video art, many artists have challenged preconceived notions of art as high priced, high-brow, and only decipherable by elite members of society. Video art is not necessarily a type of art that individuals would want to own, but rather an experience. Continuing the trend of redefining earlier ideas and ideals about art, some contemporary video artists are seeking to do away with the notion of art as a commodity. Artists turning to video have used the art form as a tool for change, a medium for ideas. Some video art openly acknowledges the power of the medium of television and the Internet, thus opening the doors of the art world to the masses.

Such artists seek to elevate the process of creating art and move beyond the notion that art should only be valued as an aesthetically pleasing product. Video art exemplifies this, for the viewer watches the work as it is actually being made; they watch as the process unfolds. Video installation pieces combine video with sound, music, and/or other interactive components. In Nicole Cohen's Please Be Seated, viewers are asked to be active participants. Using innovative video technologies, participants can sit on replicas of 18th-century French chairs and watch television screens in which they are virtually inserted in historic recreations of 18th-century French spaces. While traditional works of art are in galleries with signs that say "Do not touch," Cohen invites you to physically participate. In this way, the viewer becomes part of the work of art.

He is another artist who sought to involve the viewer, as seen in his garden at the Getty Center. In the Central Garden, which Irwin has playfully termed "a sculpture in the form of a garden aspiring to be art," viewers can experience a maze-like configuration of plants, stones, and water. Here visitors get completely immersed in the sensation of being within the work of art. The sense of smell, touch, and sound are juxtaposed with the colors and textures of the garden. All of the foliage and materials of the garden were selected to accentuate the interplay of light, color, and reflection. A statement by Irwin, "Always changing, never twice the same," is carved into the plaza floor, reminding visitors of the ever-changing nature of this living work of art. In this way, Irwin subverts the idea that a work of art should be paint on a canvas. Rather, nature can be art.

By creating a garden specifically designed for the Getty Center, Irwin engages in site-specific art. Many contemporary artists who create site-specific works move art out of museums and galleries and into communities to address socially significant issues and/or raise social consciousness. In the case of Irwin's garden and Martin Puryear's That Profile (also on view at the Getty Center), works of art are commissioned by museums to enhance and incorporate their surrounding environments. That Profile, stationed on the plaza at the foot of the stairs leading to the Museum, mimics the grid-like patterns of the Getty Center building itself. Weighing 7,500 pounds, That Profile is massive. However the work's graceful and curving lines have a "light and airy" quality that capitalizes on the surrounding mountains and ocean views visible from the Getty's plaza.

Questions such as "What is art?" and "What is the function of art?" are relatively new. Creating art that defies viewers' expectations and artistic conventions is a distinctly modern concept. However, artists of all eras are products of their relative cultures and time periods. Contemporary artists are in a position to express themselves and respond to social issues in a way that artists of the past were not able to. When experiencing contemporary art at the Getty Center, viewers use different criteria for judging works of art than criteria used in the past. Instead of asking, "Do I like how this looks?" viewers might ask, "Do I like the idea this artist presents?" Having an open mind goes a long way towards understanding, and even appreciating, the art of our own era.

CHAPTER 3: A-Z TYPES OF ART

- Animation Art

Derived from the Latin meaning "to breathe life into", animation is the visual art of creating a motion picture from a series of still drawings. Among the great twentieth century animators are J. Stuart Blackton, George McManus, Max Fleischer, and Walt Disney.

- Architecture

Best understood as the applied art of building design. Historically has exerted significant influence on the development of fine art, through architectural styles like Gothic, Baroque and Neoclassical. For the origins of skyscraper design, see: 19th Century Architecture; for its characteristics and development, see: Skyscraper Architecture (1850-present); for technical details, see: Chicago School of Architecture; for historical context, see: American Architecture (1600-present).

- Art Brut

Painting, drawing, sculpture by artists on the margin of society, or in mental hospitals, or children. (English category is Outsider art.)

- Assemblage Art

A contemporary form of sculpture, comparable to collage, in which a work of art is built up or "assembled" from 3-D materials - typically "found" objects.

- Body Art

One of the oldest (and newest) forms - includes body painting and face painting, as well as tattoos, mime, "living statues" and (most recently) "performances" by artists like Marina Abramovic and Carole Schneemann.

- Calligraphy

This fine art, practised widely in the Far East and among Islamic artists, is regarded by the Chinese as the highest form of art.

- Ceramics

A type of plastic art, ceramics refers to items made from clay and baked in a kiln. See ancient pottery from China and Greece, below. Two of the foremost European ceramicists are the English artist Bernard Howell Leach (1887-1979), and the Frenchman Camille Le Tallec (1908-91).

- Christian Art

This is mostly Biblical Art, or at least works derived from the Bible. It includes Protestant Reformation art and Catholic Counter-Reformation art, as well as Jewish themes. See also: Early Christian sculpture and also: Early Christian Art.

- Collage

Composition consisting of various materials like newspaper cuttings, cardboard, photos, fabrics and the like, pasted to a board or canvas. May be combined with painting or drawings.

- Computer Art

All computer-generated forms of fine or applied art, including computer-controlled types. Also known as Digital, Cybernetic or Internet art.

- Conceptual Art

A contemporary art form that places primacy on the concept or idea behind a work of art, rather than the work itself. Leading conceptual artists include: Allan Kaprow (b.1927), and Joseph Beuys (1921-86) the former Professor of Monumental Sculpture at the Dusseldorf Academy, whose dedication earned him a retrospective at the Samuel R Guggenheim Museum (New York).

- Design (Artistic)

This refers to the plan involved in creating something according to a set of aesthetics. Examples of artistic design movements include: Art Nouveau, Art Deco, De Stijl, Bauhaus, Ulm Design School and Postmodernism.

- Drawing

A drawing can be a complete work, or a type of preparatory sketching for a painting or sculpture. A central issue in fine art concerns the relative importance of drawing (line) versus colour.

- chalk

- charcoal

- conte crayon

- pastel

- pen and ink

- pencil

For a selection of the greatest sketches by some of the finest draftsmen in history, please see: Best Drawings of the Renaissance (1400-1550).

• Folk Art

Mostly crafts and utilitarian applied arts made by rural artisans.

• French Furniture

The greatest furniture was created during the 17th/18th centuries by French Designers at the Royal Court, in the Louis Quatorze, Quinze and Seize styles. For a short guide, see: French Decorative Arts (1640-1792).

• Graffiti Art

Contemporary form of street aerosol spray painting which emerged in East Coast American cities during the late 1960s/early 1970s. Famous graffiti artists include Jean-Michel Basquiat (1960-88), Keith Haring (1958-90) and Banksy.

• Graphic Art

Types of visual expression defined more by line and tone (disegno), rather than colour (colorito). Includes drawing, cartoons, caricature art, comic strips, illustration, animation and calligraphy, as well as all forms of traditional printmaking. Also includes postmodernist styles of word art (text-based graphics).

• Icons (Icon Painting)

Ranks alongside mosaic art as the most popular type of Eastern Orthodox religious art. Closely associated with Byzantine art, and later, Russian icon painters.

• Illuminated Manuscripts

This principally refers to religious texts (Christian, Islamic, Jewish) embellished with figurative illustrations and/or abstract geometric designs, exemplified by Book of Kells.

- Installation

A new category of contemporary art, which employs various 2-D and 3-D materials to create a particular space designed to make an impact on the viewer/visitor. Turner Prize Winner Damien Hirst and Tracey Emin are famous installation artists.

- Illustration

A form of painting, drawing or other graphic art which explains, clarifies, pictorializes or decorates written text.

- Jewellery Art

Practised by goldsmiths, as well as other master-craftsmen like silversmiths, gemologists, diamond cutters/setters and lapidaries.

- Junk Art

Artworks made from ordinary, everyday materials, or "found objects", of which Marcel Duchamp's "readymades" are a sub-category. Typically includes 3-D works like sculpture, assemblage, collage or installations.

- Land Art

A relatively new category of contemporary art, also called Earth art, earthworks, or Environmental art, it was led by Robert Smithson (1938-73), and emerged in America during the 1960s as a reaction against the commercial art world.

- Metalwork Art

Embraces goldsmithing, the fashioning of precious metals into objets d'art, as well as enamelwork techniques like cloisonné, plique-a-jour, champlevé, and encrusted enamelling. See: Celtic Metalwork. For more modern works, see also: Fabergé Easter Eggs.

- Mosaic Art

An ancient art form, developed by Ancient Greek and Byzantine artists, which creates pictorial designs out of glass tesserae. For its high point during the Middle Ages, see: Ravenna Mosaics (c.400-600) and Christian Byzantine Art (c.400-1200).

- Outsider Art

Artworks by painters/sculptors outside mainstream culture; may be mentally ill, or untutored and uneducated: (French equivalent is Art Brut).

- Painting

Since classical antiquity the highest form of Western art, painting has been dominated by Renaissance-style "Academic Art". Until the invention of pre-mixed paints and the collapsible paint tube in the mid-19th century, painters had to create their own colour pigments from natural plants and metal compounds. See colour in painting. Famous painting movements or schools include: Early/HighRenaissance, Mannerism, Baroque, Rococo, Neoclassical, Romanticism, Realism, Impressionism, Post Impressionism, Fauvism, Expressionism, Cubism, Surrealism, Abstract Expressionism, Op-Art, Pop Art, Minimalism, Photorealism, and others.

- acrylics
- encaustic painting
- fresco painting
- gouache
- ink and wash
- nail art
- oils
- miniature painting
- panel painting
- tempera painting
- watercolours
- and more

- Performance Art (and Happenings)

A 20th century art form involving a live performance by the artist before an audience. The form was explored and developed by exponents of Futurism, Constructivism, Dada, Surrealism and later contemporary art movements.

- Photography

A 20th century medium by which the artist captures pictorial images on film as opposed to the traditional fine art supports of canvas, paper or board. New computer software graphics programs have created new opportunities for editing and image manipulation. See also: Is Photography Art? Foremost among exponents of photographic art is the American Ansel Adams, a fellow of the American Academy of Arts and Sciences, a Guggenheim fellow and recipient of the Presidential Medal of Freedom, noted for his black-and-white photographs of the American West. The leading contemporary Irish lens-based artist is Victor Sloan (b.1945).

- Poster Art

Peaked during the French Belle Epoque and the Art Nouveau era.

- Primitive Art

Associated with Aboriginal, African, Oceanic and other tribal cultures; also embraces Outsider art.

- Printmaking

The process of making original prints by pressing an inked block or plate onto a receptive support surface, typically paper. Among great modern exponents of fine art printmaking (eg. woodcuts, engraving, etching, lithography and silkscreen) are the American artist James McNeill Whistler (1834–1903), the French artist Toulouse-Lautrec (1864-1901), the Dutch graphic artist MC Escher (1898-1972), Willem de Kooning (1904-97) and Robert Rauschenberg (1925-2008), as well as silkscreen printers like Andy Warhol (1928-87), all of whom infused the artform with great vitality.

- engraving
- etching
- giclee prints
- lithography
- screen-printing
- woodcuts
- and more

- Public Art

A vague category of art which encompasses all works paid for by public funds. A more narrow definition might restrict it to all works designed for a space accessible to the general public. Sadly, most public art ends up in stores or offices staffed by public servants!

- Religious Art

Typically architecture, or any fine or decorative arts with a religious theme: includes Christian or Islamic, Hindu, Buddhism or any of a hundred different sects. See for instance Chinese Buddhist sculpture (c.100 CE - present).

- Rock Art

Traditionally encompasses primitive stone engravings (petroglyphs), relief sculptures, cave painting (pictographs) and megaliths of the Stone Age.

- Sand Art

Encompasses sand painting (Navajo Indians, Tibetan Buddhists), sand drawing (Vanuatu, formerly New Hebrides), sand sculpture and architecture.

- Sculpture

Sculpture is a three-dimensional work of plastic art created either by (1) Carving - in stone, marble, wood, ivory, bone; (2) modelling - from wax or clay, after which it may be cast in bronze; (3) an assemblage of "found objects". Note: Origami paper folding should also be classed as a plastic art.

- statue

- relief sculpture

- bronze

- ice sculpture

- ivory carving

- marble

- stone

- terracotta sculpture

- wood-carving

- Stained Glass Art

The supreme decorative art of the Gothic movement, stained glass reached its zenith during the 12th and 13th centuries when it was created for Christian cathedrals across Europe. Modern stained glass was made in America by John LaFarge and Louis Comfort Tiffany; and on the Continent at the Bauhaus design school. Sadly, the creators of the stained glass masterpieces in Chartres and other Gothic cathedrals remain anonymous, however their skills were kept alive by artists like Marc Chagall

(1887-1985) and Joan Miro (1893-1983), and - in Ireland - by such Irish artists as Harry Clarke (1889-1931), Sarah Purser (1848-43) and Evie Hone (1894-1955).

- Tapestry Art

An ancient type of textile art, tapestry-making flourished in Europe from the Middle Ages onwards, at the hands of French and (later) Flemish weavers. The most famous works were woven at the Gobelins tapestry and Beauvais tapestry factories in Paris, but see also the famous Bayeux Tapestry (c.1075) a Romanesque work stitched by Anglo-Saxon and French seamsters, depicting the Norman Conquest of 1066.

- Video Art

One of the most recent categories of contemporary expression, pioneered by Andy Warhol and others, video is frequently used in installation art, as well as as a stand-alone art form. Several Turner Prize Winners have been video artists. The leading video artist of the twentieth century is probably Bill Viola (b.1951), known for his technical and creative mastery of the genre.

CHAPTER 4: BUYING ART

Why should a person purchase original art? We could all save some money and buy a cheap poster to hang in our living room or a mass-produced dew-dad to hang out on the coffee table. There are many people do the aforementioned and are quite happy. But for those of you who like to step out of the ordinary and do buy or are thinking of buying original art, here are ten fantastic reasons to buy original art.

You can buy original art simply to feel or be inspired. Art that inspires you and effects you in a meaningful way should be in your home. Not many things can inspire and make you feel like a great piece of art. Art that inspires and connects deeply with you is to be valued and be seen often. This connection allows you to share in the passion, expression, creativity and inspiration of the artist who created it. The art moves you and enhances your life.

It's certainly alright to buy original art to simply enhance and beautify your living or work space. The right piece of art and the aesthetic quality that comes with it can change the whole feeling of a room, a home, or a building. If you have a space in your life that needs a new energy, a new feel, a fresh look or a bold statement, start your search today at a local art gallery or on the web.

Some people buy original art simply for its uniqueness. A one of a kind creation is certainly unique, and you could say the owner would be somewhat unique for owning it. The piece of art can not only be unique for what it looks like, but for what it does to the people who get to see it and experience it. Or, it could be completely personal to you and no one else. A cheap poster that is just like 100,000 others just doesn't do that.

Making a statement is a great reason to buy original. Maybe a collector wants to show off their art and impress others. A show of success. Why not? People do it everyday with things far less relevant than art. There is no doubt that owning certain Art can be somewhat of a status symbol. The original art you own can also be a part of your legacy, something to leave for others when the time is right.

Buy an original piece of art to make a connection with the artist. You can look at an original painting on a wall of an artist who you know of, respect, and admire. You feel the light. You see the brush strokes.. In most cases the artist probably cares deeply about their work, and you can share in the vision and commitment. Maybe you know this artist. This artist is here with you because of that painting. You support this artist with your patronage. Your support keeps this real life artist creating more fantastic art and getting even better at their craft so you and others can share even further in the experience.

Buying original art for purely financial and investment reasons is nothing new. You are not only investing in the art, but the artist as well. While there is certainly no guarantee, some, but not all art tends to increase in value with time. That's a good thing to consider because so many of the items we buy everyday do exactly the opposite. Ever try to sell your stuff at a garage sale? That piece of clothing you bought a couple of years ago that was so in style probably isn't worth too much now.

Original art is bought for intellectual reasons too. It's been said that great or very good art advances our thoughts of who we really are and where we have been. It helps reminds us of our place in this world, or our own humanity. A certain style or school of art,the artists involved, and their attitudes on life may speak directly to you and will not let you go. The art and artists may have historical significance. This art may not speak to others but to you it's deeper than the mere surface.

Buy original art and start your own art collection. People collect all kinds of things don't they? Baseball cards, stuffed animals, die-cast cars, Barbie dolls, etc. I really don't know why people collect, they just do. The home of a serious art collector is a quite something to behold indeed.

Buy original art just because you like it. You want it. It makes you feel good. It may make you smile. You feel it was created just for you...and maybe it was. You view it every day and you feel a connection to the painting or sculpture that just makes you feel good. What's wrong with that?

If none of the above reasons work, you could always buy an original piece of art to match your carpet color or go good with your curtains.

You don't need a bunch of reasons to buy original art. Just one will do, although there are several. I personally buy art for four reasons: I love it, I'm inspired by it, I want a personal connection to the artist or the subject matter, and the desire to possess something with those qualities that is absolutely unique.

You don't have to spend a fortune to have quality art in your home. Start where you can because original art does not have to ruin your budget. Even though every so often you here about these astonishing prices for older paintings, you can start a collection at reasonable prices and see where it takes you. Your soul just might thank you for it.

Tips on buying art

1. Do your research –- Open yourself to new things and figure out what type of art you like, and the best way to do this is to see a lot of art. Visit museums and galleries, talk to other collectors and artists; try to familiarize yourself with various periods, mediums and styles.

2. Set a budget, and be prepared to spend a little more. The things that I regret most are the works that I did not buy, and for years still could not stop thinking about how much I loved the piece. Also be aware of the hidden costs of owning art: shipping, framing and insurance. If you buy something at auction, there is a buyer's premium that can be hefty.

3. Go to an auction or two before you plan on buying your first piece. Understanding the rhythm and flow of an art auction can take time and first auctions can be overwhelming. The buyer could walk away with regret if they do not properly prepare themselves.

4. Talk to other art collectors and art consultants. The art world can be overwhelming at times and speaking to experts is the best way to navigate your way through your first time purchase. You can learn a thing or two about an industry. In the art world, you can ask for a discount when purchasing from a gallery. The listed price is not always the sale price. Galleries often give discounts to collectors that have purchased several works from them already, or perhaps the gallery is interested in developing a relationship with a new prospect. When purchasing from a gallery, there is never any harm in asking, "Is that your best price?"

5. Buy what you love. Trust your heart and be confident in your purchase. Always remember it's important to try to see the piece you are considering in person. Things look different in a photograph or jpeg.

6. For the best kind of investment, consider looking into young, emerging art. These pieces are cheaper and have a great potential for increasing in value and leading to future gains. Not all art is created equal; decorative pieces or lesser pieces with impressive names can be great, but they are often times more expensive and do not appreciate for a long-term investment.

7. Keep everything -- the receipt, invoice and documentation. Don't throw anything away, as this is what is used to authenticate and value a piece.

Finally, art can be an investment but it can be a bad one. "If you are not planning on selling the art, then you're not making any money on it."

CHAPTER 5: MODERN ART

Modern art is the creative world's response to the rationalist practices and perspectives of the new lives and ideas provided by the technological advances of the industrial age that caused contemporary society to manifest itself in new ways compared to the past. Artists worked to represent their experience of the newness of modern life in appropriately innovative ways. Although modern art as a term applies to a vast number of artistic genres spanning more than a century, aesthetically speaking, modern art is characterized by the artist's intent to portray a subject as it exists in the world, according to his or her unique perspective and is typified by a rejection of accepted or traditional styles and values.

The Beginnings of Modern Art

The centuries that preceded the modern era witnessed numerous advancements in the visual arts, from the humanist inquiries of the Renaissance and Baroque periods to the elaborate fantasies of the Rococo style and the ideal physical beauty of 18th-century European Neoclassicism. However, one prevalent characteristic throughout these early modern eras was an idealization of subject matter, whether human, natural, or situational. Artists typically painted not what they perceived with subjective eyes but rather what they envisioned as the epitome of their subject.

Age Of Modernism And Art

The modern era arrived with the dawn of the industrial revolution in Western Europe in the mid-nineteenth century, one of the most crucial turning points in world history. With the invention and wide availability of such technologies as the internal combustion engine, large machine-powered factories, and electrical power generation in urban areas, the pace and quality of everyday life changed drastically. Many people migrated from the rural farms to the city centers to find work, shifting the center of life from the family and village in the country to the expanding urban metropolises. With these developments, painters were drawn to these new visual landscapes, now bustling with all variety of modern spectacles and fashions.

A major technological development closely-related to the visual arts was photography. Photographic technology rapidly advanced, and within a few decades a photograph could reproduce any scene with perfect accuracy. As the technology developed, photography became increasingly accessible to the general public. The photograph conceptually posed a serious threat to classical artistic modes of representing a subject, as neither sculpture nor painting could capture the same degree of detail as photography. As a result of photography's precision, artists were obliged to find new modes of expression, which led to new paradigms in art.

The Artist's Perspective And Modern Art

In the early decades of the nineteenth century, a number of European painters began to experiment with the simple act of observation. Artists from across the continent, including portraitists and genre painters such as Gustave Courbet and Henri Fantin-Latour, created works that aimed to portray people and situations objectively, imperfections and all, rather than creating an idealized rendition of the subject. This radical approach to art would come to comprise the broad school of art known as Realism.

Also early in the nineteenth century, the Romantics began to present the landscape not necessarily as it objectively existed, but rather as they saw and felt it. The landscapes painted by Caspar David Friedrich and J.M.W. Turner are dramatic representations that capture the feeling of the sublime that struck the artist upon viewing that particular scene in nature. This representation of a feeling in conjunction with a place was a crucial step for creating the modern artist's innovative and unique perspective.

Early Abstraction And Modern Art

Similarly, while some artists focused on objective representation, others shifted their artistic focus to emphasize the visual sensation of their observed subjects rather than an accurate and naturalistic depiction of them. This practice represents the beginnings of abstraction in the visual arts. Two key examples of this are James McNeill Whistler's Nocturne in Black and Gold: The Falling Rocket (1874) and Claude Monet's Boulevard des Capucines (1873). In the former, the artist couples large splatters and small flecks of paint to create a portrait of a night sky illuminated by fireworks that was more atmospheric than representational. In the latter, Monet provides an aerial view of bustling modern Parisian life. In portraying this scene, Monet rendered the pedestrians and cityscape as an "impression," or in other words, a visual representation of a fleeting, subjective, and slightly abstracted, perspective.

Modern Art Themes And Concepts

The history of modern art is the history of the top artists and their achievements. Modern artists have strived to express their views of the world around them using visual mediums. While some have connected their work to preceding movements or ideas, the general goal of each artist in the modern era was to advance their practice to a position of pure originality. Certain artists established themselves as independent thinkers, venturing beyond what constituted acceptable forms of "high art" at the time which were endorsed by traditional state-run academies and the upper-class patrons of the visual arts. These innovators depicted subject matter that many considered lewd, controversial, or even downright ugly.

The first modern artist to essentially stand on his own in this regard was Gustave Courbet, who in the mid-nineteenth century sought to develop his own distinct style. This was achieved in large part with his painting from 1849-1850, Burial at Ornans, which scandalized the French art world by portraying the funeral of a common man from a peasant village. The Academy bristled at the depiction of dirty farm workers around an open grave, as only classical myths or historical scenes were fitting subject matter for such a large painting. Initially, Courbet was ostracized for his work, but he eventually proved to be highly influential to subsequent generations of modern artists. This general pattern of rejection and later influence has been repeated by hundreds of artists in the modern era.

Modern Art Movements

The discipline of art history tends to classify individuals into units of like-minded and historically connected artists designated as the different movements and "schools." This simple approach of establishing categories is particularly apt as it applies to centralized movements with a singular objective, such as Impressionism, Futurism, and Surrealism. For example, when Claude Monet exhibited his painting Impression, Sunrise (1872) as part of a group exhibition in 1874, the painting and the exhibition as a whole were poorly received. However, Monet and his fellow artists were ultimately motivated and united by the criticism. The Impressionists thus set a precedent for future independently minded artists who sought to group together based on a singular objective and aesthetic approach.

This practice of grouping artists into movements is not always completely accurate or appropriate, as many movements or schools consist of widely diverse artists and modes of artistic representation. For example, Vincent van Gogh, Paul Gauguin, and Paul Cézanne are considered the principal artists of Post-Impressionism, a movement named so because of the artists' deviations from Impressionist motifs as well as their chronological place in history. Unlike their predecessors, however, the Post-Impressionists did not represent a cohesive movement of artists who united under a single ideological banner. Furthermore, the case can be made that some artists do not fit into any particular movement or category. Key examples include the likes of Auguste Rodin, Amadeo Modigliani, and Marc Chagall. Despite these complications, the imperfect designation of movements allows the vast history of modern art to be broken down into smaller segments separated by contextual factors that aid in examining the individual artists and works.

The Avant-Garde And The Progression Of Modern Art

The avant-garde is a term that derives from the French "vanguard," the lead division going into battle, literally advance guard, and its designation within modern art is very much like its military namesake. Generally speaking, most of the successful and creative modern artists were avante-gardes. Their objective in the modern era was to advance the practices and ideas of art, and to continually challenge what constituted acceptable artistic form in order to most accurately convey the artist's experience of modern life. Modern artists continually examined the past and revalued it in relation to the modern.

CHAPTER 6: HOW TO START AS AN ARTIST

(1) Practice Your Networking.

Find opportunities to meet new people, expand your professional network, and get recognized by influential players. This includes supporting other people's art, joining professional associations, organizing a panel discussion, or volunteering at a local arts organization or project. If an Emerging Leader or arts-related Meetup group doesn't exist in your town around a particular interest, start one. Find a theme and own it. Love bourbon and arts technology projects? Schedule informal gatherings at your favorite bourbon haunt and call the evenings Bourbon for Arts Infrastructure Geeks. Try hard to include people who primarily work outside of the cultural sector. The variety of viewpoints and opinions will make it a more dynamic and interesting group.

(2) Be A Well-Informed Arts Professional.

Expand your knowledge of what's happening in your desired field by signing up for newsletters, reading industry trades, and searching for applicable studies. Today's online marketplace of ideas offers a rich selection of food for thought to keep artists intellectually sated. Keep up with the daily industry news at ArtsJournal or other blogs, like Hyperallergic, find out what arts funders are thinking via Grantmakers in the Arts, curl up (virtually, of course) with some cozy arts research studies in the Create□uity Arts Policy Library, or expand your horizons and follow a non-arts resource such as Stanford Social Innovation Review. And if all that's too much, Fractured Atlas's Culture Flash newsletter offers monthly Geek Alerts for the busy artist.

(3) Be Easy To Find. Don't Be Shy!

When someone likes your work, make it easy for them to see more of it. There's no excuse not to have your own artist website tools like WordPress and Tumblr make it easy. Include a mailing list sign-up field and a donate button prominently on your site. Tell your fans about upcoming shows and projects with efficient e-newsletters from MailChimp. If you're a performer, put your Twitter handle in all program bios.

(4) Track Your Fans.

You can't build a fan base or cultivate supporters if you don't know who's seeing your work. Selling tickets with a tool like Artful.ly is valuable because it allows you to collect every ticket buyer's name whether they purchase online or at the door. Even if you don't charge for your shows, selling free tickets or taking RSVPs can help you get to know your fans. If you're not self-presenting, ask the venue for a copy of the ticket buyers' names. Aggregate your sales lists and you may discover repeat fans who could be potential donors during your next appeal.

(5) Account For Your Art-Related Expenses.

How much is your art costing you? There are many hidden expenses built into creating and presenting your work. Accounting for all of them from supplies to marketing to rehearsal, studio, or exhibition space helps you get a handle on the true cost of creating your work, which cannot only in form your pricing decisions ,but also makes it easier to create more accurate budgets and financial projections in the future. A spreadsheet program like Microsoft Excel offers an easy starting point for tracking expenses. If you're looking for something more robust, you might try Quickbooks Online or Freshbooks.

(6) Broaden Your Fundraising Horizons.

A plethora of options have cropped up to help artists raise money for their projects, including IndieGoGo, Kickstarter, and Rockethub. But you might want to consider fiscal sponsorship instead. Fiscal sponsorship allows artists to receive grants and tax-deductible contributions in ways that are normally available only to 501(c)(3) organizations. It has become an increasingly popular funding alternative for more and more artists and fiscal sponsors like Fractured Atlas can even partner with popular crowd funding websites to expand your reach while still harnessing the benefits of nonprofit status.

(7) Catalogue And Document Your Work.

Cataloging your work provides you with ready-to-go visuals for grant and residency applications, competitions, and crowd funding campaigns, as well as creating a record of your work in the event that you have to file an insurance claim. Start now by photographing everything you can and uploading it (with helpful tags and descriptions) to an online photo sharing site like Picasa and Flickr.

For the 21st-century artist, it's simply not possible to just be someone who makes art (if that ever even was the case). Now more than ever before, success requires that we be entrepreneurs and small business owners who are skilled at keeping ourselves informed networking, fundraising, and marketing our work effectively. We hope that these tips will help you make that big career leap in 2013, even if you have to do it without a jet pack.

www.ingramcontent.com/pod-product-compliance
Lightning Source LLC
Chambersburg PA
CBHW031518210526
45464CB00007B/2963